Music Class

Written by Sandra Iversen

I am going to Miss Plume's music class.
I am learning how to tune my ukulele.
I am going to sing a song in the show.

We are going to Miss Plume's music class.
We are learning a new song to sing in the show.
Miss Plume says we are cute.

microphone

I am going to Miss Plume's music class.
I am learning how to play the flute.
I am going to play my flute in the show.

We are going to Miss Plume's music class.
We are learning a new song for the show.

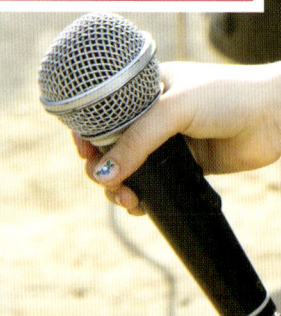

On Friday, Miss Plume's music class put on the show.

Index

drums 9
flute 7
guitar 9
microphone 5
stage 11
ukulele 3